Be the Best
GYMNASTICS

A Step-By-Step Guide

By Carey Huber

Troll Associates

Metric Equivalents

1 inch = 25.4 millimeters
or 2.5 centimeters

1 foot = 30.5 centimeters

Library of Congress Cataloging-in-Publication Data

Huber, Carey.
    Gymnastics: a step-by-step guide / by Carey Huber.
        p.   cm.—(Be the best!)
    Summary: Introduces the basics of gymnastics, from warm-up
exercises and safety tips to routines for performing on the mat,
balance beam, rings, vault, and parallel bars.
    ISBN 0-8167-1939-X (lib. bdg.)   ISBN 0-8167-1940-3 (pbk.)
    1. Gymnastics—Juvenile literature.   [1. Gymnastics.]   I. Title.
II. Series.
GV461.H78   1990
796.44—dc20   89-27394

Be the Best
GYMNASTICS

A Step-By-Step Guide

FOREWORD

by Sarah Patterson

Gymnastics is not just a sport—it's an art! A gymnast must have strength, agility, flexibility, confidence, and a sense of grace.

Gymnastics, A Step-by-Step Guide, will teach you what you need to know to get started in this wonderful sport. Keep in mind that gymnastics involves at least two important people—the gymnast as well as the coach and/or spotter.

I recommend you find a qualified gymnastics center after reading the information in this book. Then, with the help of your coach, you can discover what more and more people are discovering all the time—gymnastics is a terrific sport and a great way to exercise.

Have fun!

Sarah Patterson

Sarah Patterson is the associate athletic director and the head coach of women's gymnastics at the University of Alabama. Since 1983, her teams have consistently placed among the top finishers in NCAA championship competition. And in 1988, Sarah coached the women's gymnastics team at Alabama to both the Southeastern Conference title and the NCAA title. Sarah Patterson has won NCAA Coach of the Year honors twice, in 1986 and 1988, and is a member of the NCAA Women's Gymnastics Committee.

Contents

Introduction
To Gymnastics

Watching a skilled gymnast perform is a thrilling sight. Gymnasts gracefully flip, spin, balance, and fly through the air. To be a gymnast, you have to have strength, flexibility, agility, coordination, courage, and plenty of determination.

Why do you need determination? A gymnast is not the kind of athlete who gives up easily. A gymnastic routine that takes only minutes to perform often takes hundreds of hours of practice to master. Many times a gymnast practices the same maneuver over and over again until it can be done flawlessly. That is why a gymnast must be a determined and devoted athlete.

But gymnastics is not all work and no play. It is really lots of fun to do. Gymnastics also helps you build self-confidence and stay physically fit.

This book will show you how to have fun learning and performing basic gymnastics the correct way. Now, let's start learning about gymnastics!

The Story of Gymnastics

Some people think gymnastics is a sport developed in modern times. Gymnastics is actually a very old sport. The Chinese were practicing gymnastics as early as 2000 B.C.

Ancient Egyptians were also fond of gymnastics. Old stone carvings show Egyptians performing balance positions and other acrobatic feats.

Some ancient civilizations used forms of gymnastics to train soldiers for combat. As part of their training, Roman and Persian soldiers would jump over wooden beams similar to modern vaulting horses.

Ancient Greece was the first civilization to establish gymnastics as a formal sport. In fact, the word *gymnastics* is Greek in origin. The Greeks held gymnastic competitions in connection with their Olympic games around 776 B.C.

During Europe's Dark Ages (A.D. 400-1000) gymnastics became a forgotten activity. However, the sport was fully revived in the early 1800s. This rebirth of interest began in Sweden and Germany.

Friedrich Jahn, a German athlete, is often called the "Father of German Gymnastics." He helped develop much of the heavy apparatus, or equipment, still used in gymnastics today.

Swedish gymnasts also played a major part in resurrecting the sport. They began doing exercises that evolved into the gymnastic moves and routines of today.

From Germany and Sweden, then, the sport of gymnastics quickly spread to the rest of the world once again. Gymnastics have been a part of the modern Olympics since their inclusion at the 1896 Olympic games held in Athens, Greece. Today, gymnastics is a popular sport in most developed countries.

Preparing for Gymnastics

Before you start, get a complete physical. If you suffer from backaches or neck aches, or have a history of these problems, do *not* try the more demanding gymnastic stunts described in this book. Follow the advice of your doctor.

CLOTHING

Gymnasts usually wear tight-fitting but not restrictive clothing. Girls wear leotards. Boys wear stretch pants and tank-top shirts. Wear ballet-type slippers or go barefoot. Avoid heavy-soled sneakers. Never wear socks alone. They are too slippery and dangerous. Beginners can do fine with shorts and a T-shirt.

WARMING UP

Never try to do any gymnastic work without first warming up. If you don't warm up, you could seriously injure yourself. Your warm-up should last about twenty minutes.

A good way to start your warm-up period is to walk briskly around the gym several times. When you walk, walk like a gymnast. Be graceful. The balls, or fronts, of your feet should touch the floor first, not your heels. Walk with your head up and your stomach and rear tucked in. Take long, graceful steps.

WALK AND RUN GRACEFULLY

Head Up

Stomach And Rear Tucked In

Front Of Foot Touches Floor First

Swing Your Arms Naturally

Run Lightly On The Balls Of Your Feet

After walking, start a slow-to-moderate run. Using skipping steps, run lightly on the balls of your feet. Do not let your feet pound on the floor. Swing your arms naturally. Going around the gym a few times will increase the blood flow to your muscles and warm them up.

Flexibility
And Stretching

Flexibility is a key part of gymnastics. Everyone has different degrees of flexibility. Some people are more flexible than others. Girls are naturally more flexible than boys. However, you can increase your flexibility by regularly doing simple stretching exercises.

SITTING STRETCH

Sit on the floor with your legs together and straight out in front of you. Point your toes. Start with your hands flat on the floor at your sides. Raise your arms out to the sides until they are at shoulder level. Keep your fingers together and your hands stretched out.

SITTING STRETCH

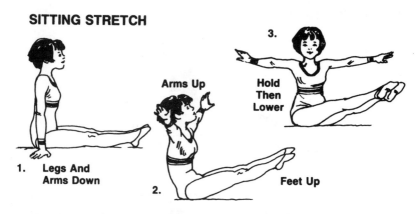

3. Hold Then Lower

Arms Up

1. Legs And Arms Down

2.

Feet Up

Now lift your feet a few inches off the floor and balance on your rear for a few seconds. Then slowly lower your arms and legs to the floor again. Remember to keep your legs straight.

SITTING BEND

Once again, sit on the floor with your legs together and straight out in front of you. With your toes pointed, lift your arms into the air above your head. Keep your fingers together, hands extended, and palms facing front. Still holding your arms in the air, slowly bend at the waist and lower your chest toward your knees. Hold this position a few seconds before rising. This is sometimes called a "long sitting." Do not bounce up and down.

SITTING BEND

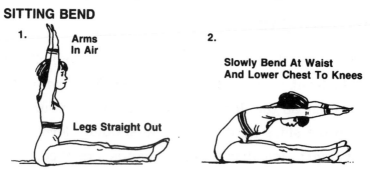

1. Arms In Air

Legs Straight Out

2. Slowly Bend At Waist And Lower Chest To Knees

STRADDLE SPLIT

This stretch is used most often by girls, though boys find it helpful, too. Sit on the floor with your legs stretched out to the sides. Point your toes. Now raise your arms above your head as you did for the sitting bend. Facing forward, bend your trunk to the side and grab your ankle with the hand to that side. Hold your ankle a few seconds, then sit back up. Bend to the other side in the same fashion. Repeat slowly.

STRADDLE SPLIT

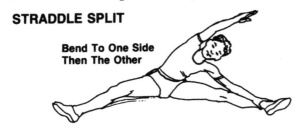

**Bend To One Side
Then The Other**

BODY RAISE

1. **Lie Flat On Stomach**

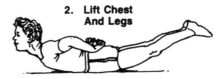

2. **Lift Chest
And Legs**

BODY RAISE

Lie on your stomach with your legs together and your toes pointed. Place your hands behind your neck or behind the small of your back (whichever you prefer). Lift your legs and chest off the floor by slowly arching your back. Then lie flat on the floor and repeat. Do this slowly.

15

BACK BRIDGE

Lie on your back on the floor. Bend your knees and bring your feet up toward your rear so your heels almost touch your bottom. Place your hands on the floor near your shoulders. Point your fingers at your feet. Now lift your torso off the floor by pushing with your arms and legs. *Do this slowly until you learn how.* Once your torso is raised, extend your arms and legs so your body forms an arch. Lean your head back. Then slowly ease your bottom back down onto the floor. Repeat.

BACK BRIDGE

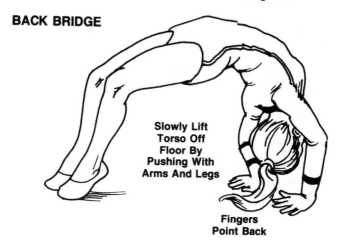

Slowly Lift Torso Off Floor By Pushing With Arms And Legs

Fingers Point Back

One caution: Do *not* try the back bridge if you suffer from back problems.

Safety

Safety is essential for beginning and advanced gymnasts alike. That does not mean you should be constantly afraid of injury. Remember, a gymnast has to be courageous. However, a good rule of thumb is: If you really are afraid of trying a maneuver, don't do it. Your own confidence affects every move you make in gymnastics.

SPOTTERS

Spotters are people who stand near the gymnast while he or she performs. A spotter is usually a coach, another gymnast, or someone who knows the sport. A spotter helps the gymnast complete a stunt if need be, and also helps safeguard against an accident. If the gymnast falls or fails to accomplish a stunt, a spotter may have to catch him or her. *Always work with a spotter.*

SAFETY BELTS

Sometimes gymnasts wear a special safety-belt harness. It goes around the gymnast's waist and has ropes attached to the sides by rings. Spotters hold the ropes. The safety-belt harness prevents a gymnast from falling while working on apparatus or doing stunts in the air.

Floor Exercises

In gymnastics, most positions and movements used in floor exercises are also adapted for use on apparatus. So it is very important to learn and master the basics of floor exercises.

MAT

The standard size of a floor-exercise mat is thirty-nine feet four and a half inches per side. It is used for both girls and boys. Floor-exercise rules require the gymnast to use the entire area of the mat. So a gymnast cannot stay in one place. He or she must move around on the mat. Usually mats are made two feet larger than the regulation area, with the competition area marked off by lines. The gymnast cannot legally go outside those lines.

PIKE POSITION

During a floor exercise, a pike position is usually done while sitting down on the mat. To get into a pike position, extend your legs straight out in front and keep them together. Point your toes. Bend at the waist, moving your knees toward your chest. Then wrap your hands around your legs. A pike position is like a tight V body position.

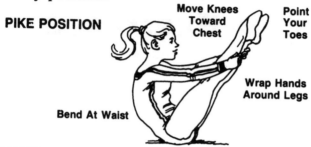

PIKE POSITION

Move Knees Toward Chest

Point Your Toes

Wrap Hands Around Legs

Bend At Waist

SPLITS

Splits are normally a part of most floor-exercise routines. However, splits are not that easy to do. Trying to force a split can result in injury. Beginners should practice splits under the watchful eyes of a coach.

The secret to a split is relaxing the muscles on the inside of the thighs enough to get the legs into a split position. Also, the hip joint must be supple enough for this to happen. A supple hip joint is why girls have an easier time doing splits than boys.

Front Split   To get into a front split position, stand with your feet flat on the floor and spread your legs about shoulder width. Keeping your legs straight, slowly slide your feet out from your body to the sides. Only go as far as is comfortable. Do not force a split. You will improve in time. As your feet go farther apart, turn your feet out so you are on the inside part of your ankles. You will eventually get down to the side of your thighs. Doing flexibility stretches (see pages 13-16) will help you improve your front splits.

FRONT SPLIT

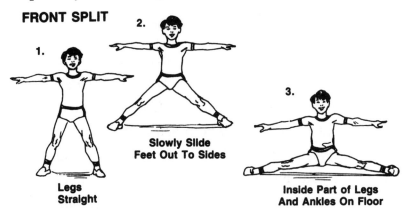

1.

Legs
Straight

2.

Slowly Slide
Feet Out To Sides

3.

Inside Part of Legs
And Ankles On Floor

Side Split This is a bit more comfortable to do than the front split. However, the side split should also be taught by a coach.

To do a side split, start in a front split (going down as far as you can go). Turn slightly toward your right leg. Gently stretch your torso to make sure you are down as far as you can go. You may have to place your hands flat

SIDE SPLIT

1.
Arms
Up

2.
Turn Torso
To Face
Right Leg

3.
Go Down
Slowly

on the floor for support. Slowly and carefully, turn your torso to the right until you are in a side split position. Your right leg should be in front of you and your left leg should be behind you.

With practice, you will be able to turn from front split to side split and back again with ease.

SUPINE ARCH, OR CRAB POSITION

A supine arch, or a crab position, is much like the back bridge position used during warm-up (see page 16). To get into a supine arch, sit on the floor, leaning back on your hands while keeping your arms straight. Now raise your body up from the floor, with your back facing the floor and your chest facing the ceiling. Keep your legs together and extended, and your head back. Your hands should be flat on the floor, and your fingers should be pointed at your feet. Keep your arms extended. Your shoulders should be above your hands.

SUPINE ARCH

1. Sit On Floor, Leaning Back On Hands
2. Raise Body Off Floor
Head Back

STRADDLE LEAN, OR TRUNK BEND

The straddle lean, or trunk bend, starts with a straddle split sitting position (see page 15). While on your bottom, spread your legs and extend them out to the sides. Rest on the inner parts of your thighs, calves, and ankles. With your arms extended up over your head, bend slowly forward and touch your chest to the floor. This is not easy and will take time to master. So be patient. Both boys and girls can do a straddle lean. It can also be done with the hands grasping the legs at the ankles.

STRADDLE LEAN

1. Arms Up

Legs Extended Out To Sides

2a. Bend Slowly Forward

Chest Flat On Floor

2b. You Can Grasp Ankles With Hands

Touch Chest To Floor

TOE RAISE

The toe raise is very simple. Stand very straight and erect with your legs and feet together. Keep your back stiff and your chin up. Extend you arms out to the sides at shoulder level. Keep your fingers together and your palms facing the floor.

Now rise up on the balls of your feet, keeping them together. Lift as high as you can. Hold that heels-up position for several seconds. Try not to wobble or shake. Then drop your heels back to the floor.

FORWARD DROP

The forward drop is a graceful fall to the floor. You start by falling frontward from a standing position. Keep your back straight. As you fall, lift one leg up behind you but keep it extended. Bring your arms out in front, with your palms facing the floor. Land lightly on your hands. Do not let your wrists slam against the mat. To cushion or break your fall, bend your arms at the elbows when your hands touch. Finish with your chin up and your back leg lifted high.

FORWARD DROP

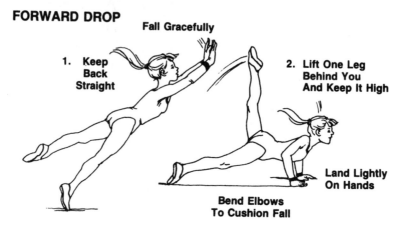

Fall Gracefully

1. Keep Back Straight

2. Lift One Leg Behind You And Keep It High

Land Lightly On Hands

Bend Elbows To Cushion Fall

SHOOT THROUGH

A shoot through is a move that is done on the floor. (It could follow a forward drop.) To do a shoot through, get in a pushup position on the floor, with your arms locked and your body raised off the mat. Keeping your arms stiff, flex your hips and bend at the waist. You'll go into a pike position (see page 20) as you swing your legs through your arms. This should be one continuous motion. Keep your head up.

Once your legs swing between your arms, you will end

up on your seat. Lean back in a sitting position with your chin up. After a shoot through, you could move into a maneuver like a supine arch (see page 22), a backward roll (see page 28), or a backward extension (see page 29).

SPECIALIZED MOVEMENTS FOR GIRLS

Two of the most popular floor movements used by girl gymnasts are the body wave and the ballet touch. Each adds grace and a bit of drama to floor routines.

Body Wave   From a toe raise position (see page 23), bend slightly forward at the waist and also bend the knees while staying balanced on your toes. As you do this, bring your arms forward so they are in front of you. Now slowly bring your arms straight down in a circular motion until they are behind your hips. As you do that, lean backward, straightening your legs and arching your back. Remember to stay balanced on your toes. Hold that position as you dramatically sweep your arms up and over your head. Finish with your back straight and your arms outstretched above your head in a Y position.

Ballet Touch   The ballet touch is a simple but graceful, dancelike movement. Stand with your feet slightly spread. Keeping one leg extended, bring it slightly forward. Bend over at the waist and bend the other knee. It is like a smooth dip forward. Reach down with the hand on the side of the extended leg to touch the extended foot. Do it gracefully. Then go back to your standing position.

Rolls

Rolls are among the most common movements used in gymnastics. They are used in floor exercises and on apparatus like the balance beam.

FORWARD ROLL (Tuck Position)

A tuck position means that your body is in a very compact position. Your chest will be tucked close to your knees as you go over.

A forward roll in a tuck position should be done on a floor-exercise mat, not on the floor itself. To do this roll, stand on the mat with your feet and legs together. Now squat down by bending your knees. Stay up on the balls of your feet. Your heels should be raised with your seat almost touching them.

Bend at the waist to put your hands flat on the mat just below and to the outside of your knees. Point your fingers forward. Your chest should be touching your knees. That is a tuck position. Try to stay in that position throughout the roll you'll be doing.

Now lower your chin so it rests against your chest. Keep your chin tucked there as you roll to avoid an injury to your neck. As you lower your head to the mat, dip your shoulders and push up with your feet. As you start to roll forward, keep your chin tucked and put the back of your head on the mat. Roll straight forward, not to one side.

FORWARD ROLL (Tuck Position)

Tuck chin into chest; knees inside hands; put weight on balls of feet.

Lower head to mat; dip shoulders; roll straight, push up with feet.

Stay tucked; grab shins as you go over.

Back up on balls of feet.

As your weight shifts to your hands, use them to push slightly. Keep your head and body tucked as you come over on your back. Shift your hands from the mat to your legs. Grab your shins. That will help you pull yourself over.

Later, after continued practice, you'll be able to do a tucked roll without grabbing your legs. As you roll forward, come back to the starting position on the balls of your feet.

BACKWARD ROLL (Tuck Position)

To do a backward roll in a tuck position, stand facing *opposite* the direction in which you will roll. Now come down into a squat position, bending your knees and tucking your chin to your chest. This time, do *not* place your hands on the mat.

Bend your arms so your hands are near the sides of your head. Bend your hands backward so your palms face upward and your fingers point behind you. From the squat position, roll backward by pushing slightly with your feet. Keep your body tucked. Go straight over, not to the side. As you roll backward, your hands will be in position to place your palms flat on the mat. Keep your elbows in and push firmly with your hands to lift your head and shoulders off the mat. Keep your legs together and knees tucked to your chest. Bring your feet back under your body as you finish the roll to resume the starting stance.

BACKWARD ROLL (Tuck Position)

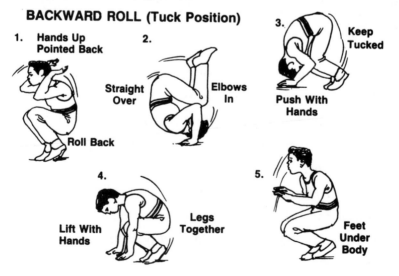

1. Hands Up Pointed Back
   Roll Back

   Straight Over

2. Elbows In

3. Keep Tucked
   Push With Hands

4. Lift With Hands
   Legs Together

5. Feet Under Body

FORWARD ROLL (Straddle Position)

The forward roll in a straddle position is started from a standing rather than a squat position. Stand with your feet spread well apart (beyond shoulder width). Lock your legs at the knees and point your toes outward.

Bend at the waist and put your hands flat on the mat about shoulder width. Tuck your chin to your chest. Your weight should now be on your hands.

Shift your weight to the front by leaning forward. Lower your head and shoulders to the mat as you would in a regular forward roll. The straddle roll is like a forward roll except for the position of your legs. They should remain in a straddle or V position as you roll over.

As you start to come forward, shift your arms and hands back into the start position (rather than grab your shins as in a forward roll, tuck position, described on pages 26-27). Use your hands to push yourself up to return to the standing start position.

BACKWARD EXTENSION

The backward extension is a variation of a backward roll. It is a bit difficult but looks very impressive. To start a backward extension, get into the starting position for a backward roll (see page 28). Do a backward roll up to the point where you push yourself over with your hands. This is the point where the stunt changes. Instead of rolling over backward and staying in a tuck position, you push up and extend your legs straight up into the air. It is like rolling over backward into a handstand position.

To do a backward extension well, you must shoot your legs straight up into the air and push up hard with your arms and hands. Keep your legs together and your toes pointed. Hold the handstand position for a second. Finish by whipping your feet out and downward toward the mat. This way, you'll end in a standing position.

DIVE ROLL

The dive roll is an advanced stunt that should only be tried with the help of a coach. It can be started from a standing still position or a run-and-jump takeoff.

To do a dive roll from a standing position, place your feet together. What you are going to do is spring forward by pushing off with your feet and then dive toward the mat. As you dive, bend at the waist. Keep your chin tucked, and make sure your arms are at least shoulder width apart. Pretend you are diving over something in your path.

Your hands will hit first and cushion your impact. Then your hips will come forward. With your chin still tucked, bring your legs and knees in as you start to roll over. Bend your knees as you roll. If you don't get your knees in, your legs will slap against the mat. Once you're on the mat, the roll is just another forward roll (see page 26). The momentum of your dive should carry you to your feet.

Other Moves

There are several basic floor-exercise moves that can also be used in vaulting, on the balance beam, and on other apparatus. Mastering these moves will prepare you to learn more difficult stunts in the future.

CARTWHEEL

The cartwheel is a sideways handspring. The arms and legs stay spread like the spokes of a bicycle wheel. A cartwheel can be done to either side.

To do a cartwheel, stand sideways with your feet spread shoulder width or a bit wider. Extend your arms outward from your body and just above your shoulders. Your arms and torso should look like the letter Y.

CARTWHEEL

1. **2. Shift Weight To One Side** **3. Kick Up**

Arms And Legs Spread

Reach Down

Keep Legs Spread

4.

Keep Back Straight

5.

Shift Weight

6.

Return To Starting Position

To cartwheel to the left, shift your weight slightly to your right foot as you raise your left, and step out sideways to the left. Point your toe as you step.

As the left foot comes down, reach downward toward the mat with your extended left arm. Do not bend at the elbow. As you go down, kick up and over your body with the right leg. Do not let it bend. Your weight is shifted to your left leg and hand. The right hand follows down and touches the mat as your legs start to go up and over. Keep your legs straight and split as they go over your body. Keep your arms straight, too.

Your momentum will carry you over. Keep your back straight. Do not let your hips droop. The legs must carry straight over the body and not to the side.

As your legs swing down, push off with your hands. Your right leg will touch first and carry you into your starting position.

ROUND-OFF

A round-off is a little like a cartwheel. To do a round-off, take a short run approach straight in (not to the side). Your body should face frontward. Take a short hop-step. As you do, change the direction of your body from facing frontward to sideward. Dive to the mat with your arms extended, reaching for the floor (like a cartwheel). Push off with your left foot as you kick up your right leg over your body.

With both hands on the mat, bring your legs up into a handstand position (sideways). After you get into this

ROUND-OFF

1. Face Front
Running Approach
Hop-Step

2. Face Sideward And Reach For Floor
Kick Up

3. Legs Together

4. Push Off With Hands
Quarter Turn In Air

5. Snap Legs Down

handstand position, your body should make a quarter turn in the air as you snap your legs downward toward the mat. This rounding off is how the stunt got its name. As your legs snap downward, push off the mat with your hands. Your body will sail through the air, turn, and end up landing so that you'll be facing the direction from which you came.

FRONT WALKOVER

The front walkover is a graceful maneuver mostly used by girl gymnasts. Make sure you use a spotter for this stunt.

Begin from a standing position. Raise your arms straight above your head and keep them extended. Now stride forward, lifting your left leg. Your weight should be on your right foot. As your left foot touches the mat, shift your weight forward as you bend and reach for the mat with *both* hands. Your hands should both touch at once. Kick up and straight over your right leg. Keep your body straight. It should not turn as it does in a cartwheel or a round-off.

In a front walkover, your legs should not come together in a handstand position in the air. They stay apart. Your right leg comes over first, with your left leg following in a wide split. The wider your legs are apart, the better your front walkover will be.

Your right leg should continue all the way over, trailed by your left leg. When your right leg touches the mat, your body will appear to be in a one-leg supine arch (see page 22). As your right foot touches, push off with your hands. Your left leg will then come down and touch the mat, providing the momentum to carry your body over. Your torso will be bent as your hands come forward over your body. You'll finish in a starting position.

FRONT WALKOVER

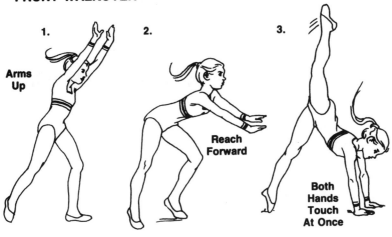

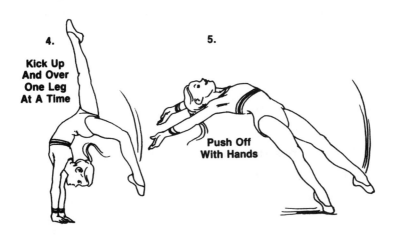

Balance Positions

In floor exercises and on apparatus, balance positions are used between various stunts in a gymnastic routine. They provide a change of pace and add grace to a performance.

BALANCE SEAT

The balance seat is sometimes called a V seat. It is not too difficult. Sit on the mat with your legs extended straight out in front. Put your arms straight out to the side at shoulder level. Keeping your legs and feet tightly together, lift your legs into the air. Lift them up so your straight legs and back form a perfect V shape. Hold that position while balancing on your seat.

ONE-LEG BALANCE

The one-leg balance can be done on either foot. Put one foot flat on the floor. Slowly raise the other leg out to the side as high as you can. Remember to keep it extended with toes pointed. Once it is up as high as it will go, grasp the instep part of the raised foot with the hand to that side. Gracefully raise the other arm into the air above your head. Make sure it is extended with the palm in. Hold the one-leg balance position for several counts.

ONE-LEG BALANCE

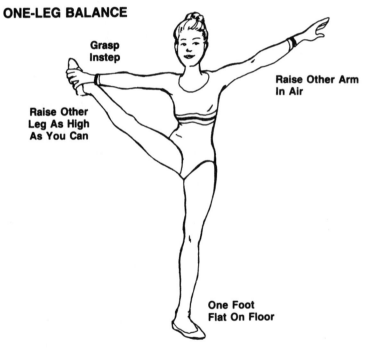

Grasp Instep

Raise Other Arm In Air

Raise Other Leg As High As You Can

One Foot Flat On Floor

FRONT SCALE

A front scale is a balance position done on one foot. Usually people are more comfortable doing it on the right foot.

To do a front scale, put your right foot flat on the mat. Keep your right leg straight. As you bend forward at the waist, lift your left leg up into the air behind you. Get the heel as high as you can and point the toes. Keep your chin up and reach out forward with both arms extended palms down.

FRONT SCALE

Reach Out
With Arms

Lift Left Leg
Behind You

Bend
At Waist

Right Foot
Flat On Mat

NEEDLE SCALE

A needle scale is also a one-foot balance position requiring good flexibility. It can be done on either foot.

If you decide to do a needle scale on your left foot, place it flat on the floor. Now bend forward at the waist. As you do, lift your right leg up behind you. Both legs must remain straight. Do not bend at the knees.

Now bend all the way over so your chest is against your left knee. Place your hands flat on the floor and extend your right leg straight up. It should look like a needle.

The needle scale takes a great deal of practice to master. You must be very flexible to accomplish it (see pages 13-16).

SQUAT BALANCE

To get into a squat balance position, stand on the mat with your feet spread about shoulder width. Your heels should be in and your toes out. Bend at the knees but do not keep your legs and knees together. Have your knees spread like a baseball catcher's.

Place the palms of your hands flat on the mat inside your legs. Keep your palms apart. Your elbows should touch the insides of your knees, and your fingers should point forward and be spread.

Lean forward slowly, rising up on your toes. Balance yourself on your hands. As you balance yourself, lift your toes off the mat, keeping your head up. Press down on your fingers to get your balance. Spread your fingers to give yourself a better base for balancing.

HEAD STAND

Squat down on the mat as you did to get into the starting position for the squat balance. What you will do in a head stand is make a support triangle between your hands and the top of your forehead. Have a spotter standing by.

As you lean forward onto your hands, place your forehead on the mat about ten inches from your fingertips.

HEAD STAND

1. Place Forehead On Mat As You Lean Onto Hands

2. Legs Rise

3. Legs Rise Straight Up

Rise on your toes and then lift your feet off the ground. Your weight should be on your hands more than your head at this point. You must keep your neck tense and rigid to avoid injury. As your legs rise, your weight will be equally distributed between the triangle formed by your hands and head.

Make sure you are balanced by holding a pike position (see page 20) for a second or so before lifting your legs straight up into the head stand. Your hips should be in a straight line with your shoulders. If your hips go too far forward, you will fall.

A spotter can help by supporting your legs once you're up. You can also practice against a wall, touching it with your feet for support when up. (For this, a spotter is a must.) Come back down by lowering one foot to the mat, then the other.

HANDSTAND

The handstand is a key balance position in gymnastics. A good way to learn it is to practice against a wall. Facing the wall, place your hands on the floor about four inches away from the wall. Keep your hands about shoulder width apart. Spread your fingers to provide a better base for balancing.

Position your shoulders just above your hands. If your shoulders are behind your hands, you will have trouble getting up. If they are beyond them, you will fall over.

Kick up one leg or both legs at once. As you go up, keep your arms straight. The back of your head should come to rest against the wall and your heels should barely touch the wall.

Have a spotter watch you and help you. Your toes should be pointed and your legs should be as straight as possible. Arch your back only slightly; tightening your hip muscles will help. Keep your shoulders directly above your hands.

Concentrate on your balance while practicing the handstand. Use your fingers to gain balance by applying pressure on them. As your technique and balance improve, start your handstand a little farther away from the wall. Eventually, you won't need it for support. But be sure to have a spotter standing by.

FOREARM STAND

The forearm stand is similar to the handstand. The difference is in the base. Instead of just the hands, the entire forearm is used.

Place your hands and forearms flat on the mat. Your fingers should be spread and your elbows shoulder width apart. Angle your hands toward each other so your thumbs touch.

The kick up into the balance position is the same one used in the handstand. Remember to keep your head up. The back arch in the balance position is slightly greater in the forearm stand than in the handstand. Come down by lowering one foot at a time to the mat. Once again, use a spotter.

Springs

Springs lift you off the floor and propel you into the air. Creating momentum as you go into a spring and riding it to the end are the keys to doing a successful spring.

HEAD SPRING

The head spring is the basic spring used in gymnastics. Gaining good height as you spring into the air is necessary for a successful landing. So beginners usually first learn to spring from an elevated or raised base rather than from the flat floor. A good elevated base to use is a small, padded gymnastics mat that has been rolled up tightly like a jelly roll. Be sure to use a spotter.

Before trying a head spring, make sure there's ample mat in front of you to do it. Then place your hands shoulder width apart and flat on the mat. Put your forehead on the mat about eight inches from your fingertips.

This is like the tripod position for a head stand (see page 40).

Keep your legs straight and together behind you and rise up on your toes. Lift your feet off the mat, placing your body in a pike position (see page 20). Roll your hips over your head while keeping your feet close to the mat. As you begin to feel your hips roll forward, whip your feet and legs upward and forward. That will get your body into an arch position in the air. While this is happening, push off hard with your hands. The whip of your legs and push of your hands will provide the spring. As your feet come to the floor, remain in an arch position and flex your knees to cushion the landing. Try to land with your feet close together.

HEAD SPRING

HANDSPRING

Like a round-off, a handspring is started with a short running approach. When you try a handspring, use a spotter. And be sure there's enough mat in front of you to do it.

Approach the mat at a moderate speed to gain momentum. Know the spot you plan to spring from in advance, and concentrate. With palms flat, throw both hands to the mat by reaching out three or four feet in front of the lead leg. Keep your hands shoulder width apart. One leg should be forward, with your knee near your chest, and the other should be farther back.

Kick your back leg up and over hard as you push off with your front leg. The legs are not together but apart (somewhat like a walkover), with the front leg trailing the back leg. As your body goes over the shoulders, push off hard with the hands. Your body will then arch over and downward. Land lightly on the leg that was kicked over first. Your other leg will follow. Keep your arms straight throughout the stunt, including the finish.

HAND SPRING

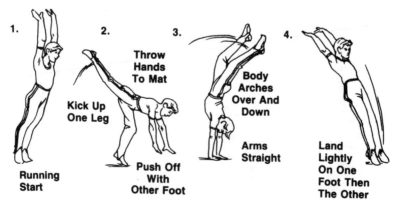

1. Running Start

2. Kick Up One Leg — Throw Hands To Mat — Push Off With Other Foot

3. Body Arches Over And Down — Arms Straight

4. Land Lightly On One Foot Then The Other

44

Balance Beam

The balance beam is used only by girl gymnasts in competition. As its name suggests, many maneuvers on it are basically balance positions like those described on pages 48-50. However, rolls and other stunts like walkovers are also commonly performed on the balance beam. Two important rules of the balance beam are not to fall off and never get on without a spotter nearby.

THE BEAM

The balance beam is sixteen feet four and seven-eighths inches long, and it is four inches wide. A competition beam is forty-seven and a quarter inches above the floor. Training beams can be lower. There are always mats under the beam, and a spotter is a must.

MOUNTS

A mount is a specialized, graceful or acrobatic way of getting on a piece of apparatus.

Front Support Mount This is probably the easiest mount to learn. With your arms at your sides, stand facing the side of the beam. Place both hands on the beam about shoulder width apart. Bend your knees and spring to a position where your arms support your weight and the fronts of your thighs rest on the beam. Hold your chin up and point your toes.

FRONT SUPPORT MOUNT

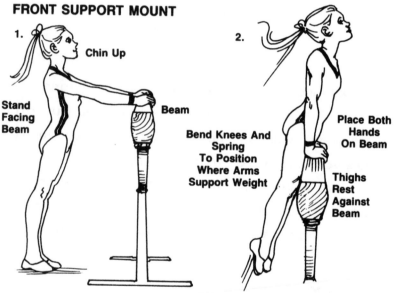

1.
Chin Up
Stand Facing Beam
Beam
Bend Knees And Spring To Position Where Arms Support Weight

2.
Place Both Hands On Beam
Thighs Rest Against Beam

One Knee Mount This mount begins just like the front support mount. Face the side of the beam and spread your hands on it about shoulder width. Spring up, supporting your weight on your hands, and place one knee on the beam. Your other leg should be stretched out very straight behind you.

46

ONE KNEE MOUNT

SQUAT MOUNT

Other Leg Straight Out Behind You

1. Put Hands On Beam

Squat Position

2.

With Hands On Beam, Spring Up So That One Knee Is On Beam.

Running Approach

Leap Up So Both Feet Land On Beam

Squat Mount This mount starts with a running two- to three-step approach from the side. Run toward the side of the beam and spread your hands shoulder width. Put your hands on the beam and leap up so both your feet land on it. Your body should be in a squat position. Time your run so your momentum does not cause you to fall over the other side of the beam.

Step-Up Mount This is another mount that uses a running approach. This time, don't run directly at the beam, but run alongside it. Run so your right side is nearest the beam. After several quick steps, take off on your left foot and lift your right knee high in the air along the beam's side. Throwing your left arm up will help you gain height. Place your right hand on the beam to steady yourself as you lift your right foot and then bring your other foot onto the beam. Use your arms for balance.

MOVEMENTS ON THE BEAM

Many of the stunts, movements, and balance positions described in the floor-exercise section (see pages 19-25) can be performed on the balance beam. To put together a balance beam routine, combine a series of movements that naturally flow from one into the other. Remember, even simply walking the beam should be done in a graceful, interesting way.

Always try to keep your body straight and your toes pointed. Let your arms swing freely or hold them in the correct balance stance. Running on the beam adds drama. If you do so, take short, almost playful steps and motions. Use turns and direction changes to add variety to your performance.

Pivot Turn   Also called the tiptoe turn, it is the simplest of all turns. Stand on the beam with the heel of one foot in front of the toe of the other. Rise up on the balls of your feet and pivot to the same side as your back foot until your toes face in the opposite direction.

Squat Turn   This is actually just a pivot turn in a different position. Instead of standing straight up, squat down on the beam with your knees close to your chest. Then do the exact same maneuver as described in the pivot turn.

Pirouette   This is a graceful turn done on *one* foot. Stand on one foot on the beam. Raise your arms above your head for balance. Hold them in a graceful pose.

SQUAT TURN

Arms In Front

Squat On Beam

Spin On Balls Of Feet

PIROUETTE

Raise Arms For Balance

Other Knee High

Rotate On One Foot

Lift the other leg until the knee is about waist high. Keep your toes pointed. Then rotate on the ball of the foot on the beam to make the turn.

Stride Leap Start at one end of the balance beam. Take a quick stride forward down the beam. As the front of your lead foot touches the beam, swing your other leg forward along the side of the beam and spring up into the air. It is a one-foot takeoff. As you reach the top of your leap, keep your legs scissored apart as in a side split (see page 21). Landing and keeping your balance is difficult. So keep your arms outstretched to help you balance as you land on one foot first. Concentrate and always use a spotter.

Jump-Off Dismount Stand gracefully on the beam with your two feet facing the side. Then just jump off the beam and land gracefully, keeping your knees and legs together and arms extended out to the sides. Arch your back and keep your chin up.

Front Vault Dismount Assume a pushup position on the beam. The insides of your palms should touch, with your fingers down opposite sides of the beam. Your hands should be below your shoulders. Keep your chin up. Then drop one leg off the beam and swing it back up hard. At the same time, lean forward on your hands and arch your back. Now kick your other leg up. Your feet should swing high up together behind your legs. Shift your weight to the side, and push off with your hands. Drop to a landing and stay facing the length of the beam. Keep your inside hand on the beam for support.

FRONT VAULT DISMOUNT

1. Push Up Position
Chin Up
Drop One Leg Off Beam And Swing It Up Hard

2. Swing Feet Up Behind You Together
Push Off With Hands

3. Arm On Beam
Side Of Body Faces Beam
Drop To A Landing

Vaulting

Soaring over a vaulting horse is one of the most exciting feelings in gymnastics. Vaulting may *look* hard. But most vaults are really not that hard to learn. They take good timing, concentration, and plenty of practice with a qualified coach.

VAULTING HORSE

The body of the vaulting horse is about five feet three inches long and fourteen to sixteen inches wide. It is held up by two support stands. The horse is padded and covered with leather or vinyl.

For vaulting competition, the horse is about four feet four inches high for men and three feet seven inches high for women.

Male gymnasts vault the length of the horse. Female gymnasts vault the width of the horse.

SPRINGBOARD

A springboard, or beat board, is used for the takeoff in vaulting. It is a small, springy, wooden board that adds height to the vaulter's takeoff.

MATS

Mats on the landing side of the vaulting horse are normally double or triple the thickness of regular floor-exercise mats.

APPROACH

Vaulting always begins with a long, swift running approach. Concentration is important, and so is knowing your exact takeoff spot. The springboard must be hit just right to insure success. In approaching the horse, all your strides should be of equal length. Again, always work with a coach while you learn how to vault.

SQUAT VAULT

In the squat vault, you'll go over the horse with your body in a squat or tuck position. Get a good running start. Hit the springboard with both feet. When you do, bend your knees. Spring forward and up, driving your hips into the air. With palms flat, place your hands about shoulder width apart on the horse. Point your fingers forward, *not* out to the sides. Keep your arms straight.

SQUAT VAULT

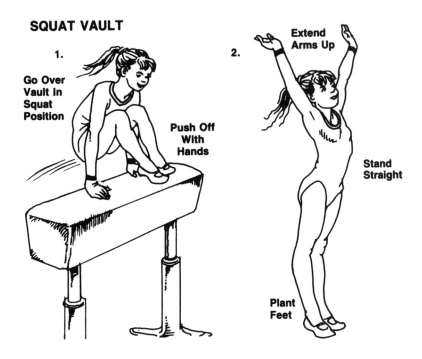

1.

Go Over
Vault In
Squat
Position

Push Off
With
Hands

2.

Extend
Arms Up

Stand
Straight

Plant
Feet

As your hands touch the horse, draw your knees up into your chest. Swing your legs through your arms, then up and over the horse. Push off with your hands. Straighten your body as you come down to land. Try to land and plant your feet in one spot without taking any steps forward or backward. Flex your knees to absorb the shock of landing without shifting. Then stand straight with your arms up and extended.

STRADDLE VAULT

The straddle vault is quite similar to the squat vault. The difference between them is the body position over the horse. Your legs will be spread wide in a straddle position.

STRADDLE VAULT

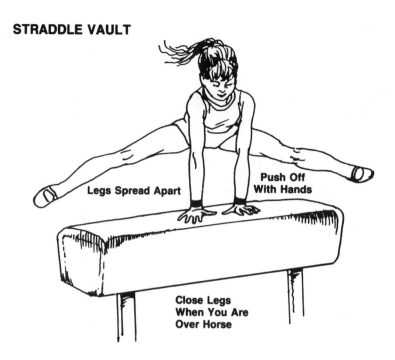

Legs Spread Apart

Push Off With Hands

Close Legs When You Are Over Horse

After your approach run and takeoff from the springboard, drive your hips very high. As you reach out and touch the horse, spread your legs wide and keep them straight. When your spread legs clear the horse, push off with your hands. Snap your legs together once you are over the horse. Land with your feet and legs together. Hold your arms high, arch your back, and keep your chin up. Remember, try not to take any steps.

Even Parallel Bars

The even parallel bars are used only by men in competition. But a number of women enjoy working out on the even parallel bars informally.

The even parallel bars are two smooth wooden rails about shoulder width apart and supported by uprights on a sturdy base. They are eleven and a half feet long and usually five and a quarter feet from the ground. Their height can be adjusted for beginners. *Never* do any work on the parallel bars without the assistance of spotters and a coach.

GRIP

Beginners should use an overhand grip on the even parallel bars. To grip the bars, stand at one end with your body in the middle. Put one hand on top of each bar, keeping your thumbs on the insides and your other fingers on the outsides of the bars.

JUMP MOUNT TO STRAIGHT-ARM SUPPORT

The jump mount is the simplest and easiest mount to learn. Stand at the end of the bars with your body in between them. Use the overhand grip.

Flex slightly at the knees and jump straight up. As you do, lift with your arms until they are fully extended. Once your arms are fully extended, lock them at the elbows. This is how you'll support yourself in the air. Arch your back and keep your legs straight, with your toes pointed down. The locked-elbows position is called a straight-arm support position.

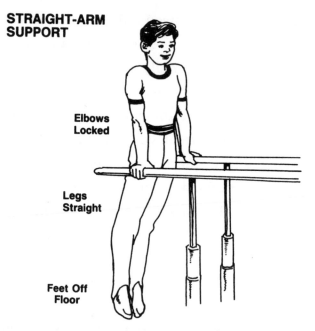

STRAIGHT-ARM SUPPORT

Elbows Locked

Legs Straight

Feet Off Floor

STRAIGHT-ARM SUPPORT TRAVEL

Once you are in a straight-arm support, try traveling down the bars. What you do is shift your weight from side to side. As you shift your weight to the right, advance your left hand a bit down the bar. Regain your grip with the left hand and shift your weight left. Then advance your right hand a bit. This way, you travel down the length of the bars bit by bit.

When you shift your weight to an arm, keep it straight and your elbow locked. Only the arm moving down the bar should be flexed.

SWING

A swing on the even parallel bars is done from a straight-arm support. Make sure you have a good grip. Start slowly by swinging your feet slightly back and then forward. Gradually increase the arch of your swing until your legs are parallel with the bars at the peak of your back and front swing. Keep your legs and feet together and your toes pointed. Always use a spotter.

SWING AND STRADDLE

Start at the end of the bars. Use a jump to a straight-arm support. Start to swing. When your forward swing is high enough that your legs are above the bars, you are ready for this maneuver.

Once your legs rise up above the bars, spread your legs into a straddle (a leg on the outside of each bar). Straddle the bars so you are in a sitting position. Your hands should still be behind you. While in the straddle, lean forward and release your grip. Reach forward with both hands at once and regrip the bars in front of you.

Kick your legs back and up off the bars behind you. Bring your legs together as they sail above the bars, then swing them forward between the bars. At the top of the forward swing, straddle the bars again. Repeat the same procedure all the way down the bars. Remember to keep your legs and arms straight.

FORWARD ROLL TO STRADDLE

Start on the bars in a straddle seat (see page 57) with your hands *forward*. Also lean your head and shoulders forward. Your head will go through the bars, and your shoulders will touch the bars, preventing you from falling through. Place your shoulders on the bars six to eight inches in front of your hands.

FORWARD ROLL TO STRADDLE

Straddle Seat

Shoulders Touch Bars

Roll Over Into Pike Position

Legs Apart

1. Head, Shoulders And Hands Forward

2. Head Goes Between Bars

3. Release Grip Elbows Out

4.

As you roll forward, make sure your elbows are pressed outward away from your body. This will help you roll and also keep you from falling through. As your hips roll over your body, release your grip while keeping your elbows out. Bring your hands forward, then roll over into a pike position (see page 20).

Once you start to roll over, regain your grip on the bars. Grab the bars in front of the roll and return to the straddle seat with hands forward.

FRONT SUPPORT TURN

Begin in a straight-arm support position in the middle of the bars. If you want to turn to the right, shift your weight and hips to the right side. You should lean in this direction but keep your body straight. Lift your left hand off the left bar and bring it over to the right bar.

Now shift your weight quickly to your left hand. Lean a bit forward over the bar so your thighs rest against it. That will help support you.

Continue the turn by taking your right hand off the right bar and quickly reaching back across to grasp the left bar. Once this is done, you will be in a straight-arm support facing the opposite direction.

SHOULDER STAND

Start in a front straddle seat position (see page 57). Roll forward as in the forward roll (see page 58), with your elbows pressed out from your body. Your shoulders should be about eight inches away from your hands.

When your hips are above your head in a pike position, raise your legs very slowly. They should remain apart until they are overhead and in line with your body. Then bring your legs together and point your toes. Keep your back arched and your chin up.

SHOULDER STAND

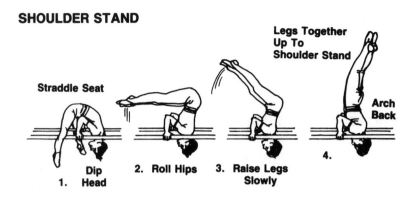

Straddle Seat

Legs Together Up To Shoulder Stand

Arch Back

Dip
1. Head

2. Roll Hips

3. Raise Legs Slowly

4.

DISMOUNTS

As already discussed for the balance beam (see pages 49-50), the dismount is a graceful or acrobatic way of getting off a piece of apparatus. The following are three standard dismounts from the even parallel bars.

Shoulder Stand and Side Fall Dismount Start in a shoulder stand position (see page 59). Lean your body to the side of the bars you wish to dismount from (in this case, to the right). As you do this, gently push away from the bar with your left hand.

SHOULDER STAND AND SIDE FALL DISMOUNT

1. Lean To Side You Want To Dismount From

2. Let Go

Fall To Side

3. Turn Hand On Bar

4. Stand Straight

Hand On Bar

Allow your body to fall to the right while in an upright straight position. As your right shoulder starts to come away from the bar, turn your right hand on the bar as you land. Finish with your right hand on the bar and your body standing very straight. You should be facing down the bars.

Rear Dismount   A rear dismount to the right is done at the peak of a forward swing. As your legs swing up over the bar, take your left hand off the left bar and bring it over to the right bar in front of your right hand. Then release your right hand from the bar as your legs go over the bar and come down to land on the mat to the right. (Reverse this sequence if you want to dismount on the left side.)

REAR DISMOUNT

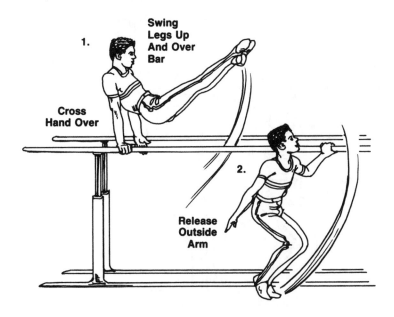

Front Dismount   A front dismount to the left is done at the peak of a backward swing. As your legs fly up over the bars behind you, take your right hand off the right bar. Move it over to grab the left bar in front of your left hand. Swing your legs over the left bar. As your legs come down, release your left hand from the left bar. Your right hand remains on the bar to provide support as you drop your legs on the mat for the landing. Remember to keep your legs straight until both feet touch the ground.

FRONT DISMOUNT

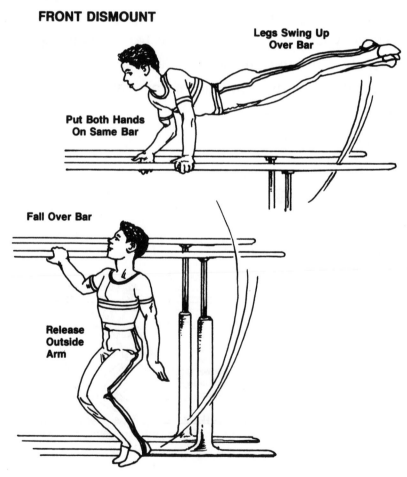

Safe Gymnastics Fun

Gymnastics is fun, exciting, and hard work. And the sport of gymnastics is constantly improving. New and more difficult stunts and maneuvers are being added regularly.

The two keys to beginning gymnastics are safety and confidence. Never work alone; always use a spotter. Also, follow the advice of a coach. After helping you to master the gymnastic events described in this book, your coach can then teach you how to use other apparatus. These apparatus often are more difficult to learn and require advanced training in technique. For boys, that would be the rings, pommel horse, and horizontal bars. For girls, that would be the uneven parallel bars.

But no matter what apparatus you choose or how many, *believe* in your ability. And practice, practice, practice. If you do, who knows? Someday you may be good enough to compete in the Olympics!

INDEX